Pies in the Sky

By Cameron Macintosh

“Hi, Ty!” called Vi.
“Hop in the pie pod!”

Ty said, “Will we drive?”

“No, let’s fly,” said Vi. “We must get that box of pies to Sam while they are hot.”

Vi set the pod mode to "flight". The pod lifted up to the sky.

"The flight should be quick," said Ty.

When the pie pod got up high,
Vi and Ty got a fright.

It was a sky jam!

"There are so many pods up here!" said Vi. "We will be late!"

"Shall we drive?" said Ty.

"Why not?" sighed Vi.

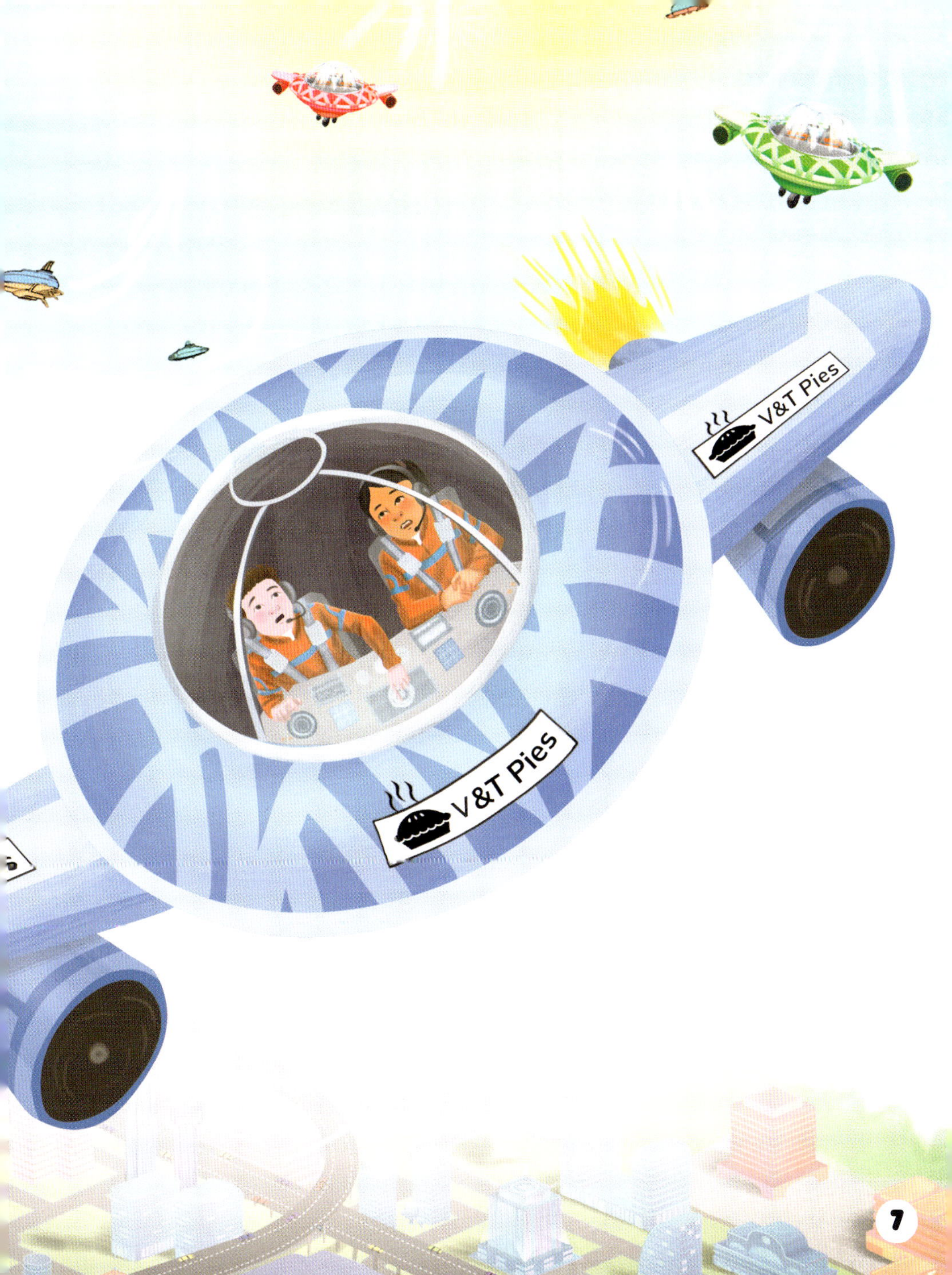
V&T Pies
V&T Pies

Bit by bit, the pod came down from the sky.

“I can land on that highway,” said Ty.

“Yes, right on that bit!” said Vi.

Ty landed the pie pod on the highway.

Vi set the pod mode to "drive".

That was a top landing, Ty!
Let's get these pies to Sam.

“We must get to Sam’s home by the time the sunlight fades,” said Vi.

"Are the pies still hot?" said Vi.

"They are just right!" said Sam.

Vi and Ty gave wide smiles.

CHECKING FOR MEANING

1. What happened after Vi set the pod mode to "flight"? *(Literal)*
2. What did Ty and Vi decide to do when they saw the traffic jam in the sky? *(Literal)*
3. Why did Vi and Ty smile widely at the end of the story? *(Inferential)*

EXTENDING VOCABULARY

sighed	Read the word *sighed*. How might you be feeling if you *sighed*?
highway	Which letters in the word *highway* make the long /ī/ sound? What is the difference between a highway and the street where you live?
fades	What is the base of the word *fades*? What is happening if the sunlight is fading? Is it getting lighter or darker?

MOVING BEYOND THE TEXT

1. What do you think it would be like to ride in the pie pod? Would it be better than a car or bus? Why?
2. Have you ever eaten a pie? What filling did it have?
3. Ty and Vi came up with a new plan when there was a traffic jam in the sky. This is called problem-solving. Why is it important to be able to solve problems or come up with a new plan?
4. If you had a pod that could drive *and* fly, where would you go in it? Why?

TIME TO WRITE

Write about a time when something didn't go the way you planned. Describe what happened and how you solved the problem.

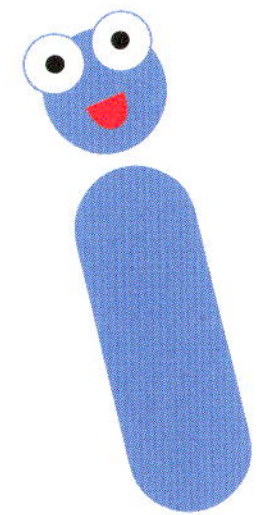

PRACTICE WORDS

hi

Ty

Vi

pie

fly

pies

flight

sky

I

highway

why

sunlight

right

fright

high

sighed

by